Eyewonder

Shark

LONDON, NEW YORK,
MELBOURNE, MUNICH, and DELHI

Written and edited by Fleur Star
Designed by Gemma Fletcher
and Sophie Pelham

Art director Rachael Foster
Publishing manager Bridget Giles
Picture researcher Liz Moore
Production editor Sean Daly
Production controller Pip Tinsley
Jacket designer Natalie Godwin
Jacket editor Mariza O'Keeffe

Consultant Dr. Trevor Day

First published in the United States in 2009 by
DK Publishing
375 Hudson Street, New York, New York 10014

10 11 12 13 10 9 8 7 6 5 4
ED809—02/09

A catalog record for this book
is available from the Library of Congress.

ISBN 978-0-7566-5225-8 (Hardcover)
ISBN 978-0-7566-5224-1 (Library Binding)

Printed and bound in Italy by L.E.G.O.

Discover more at
www.dk.com

Contents

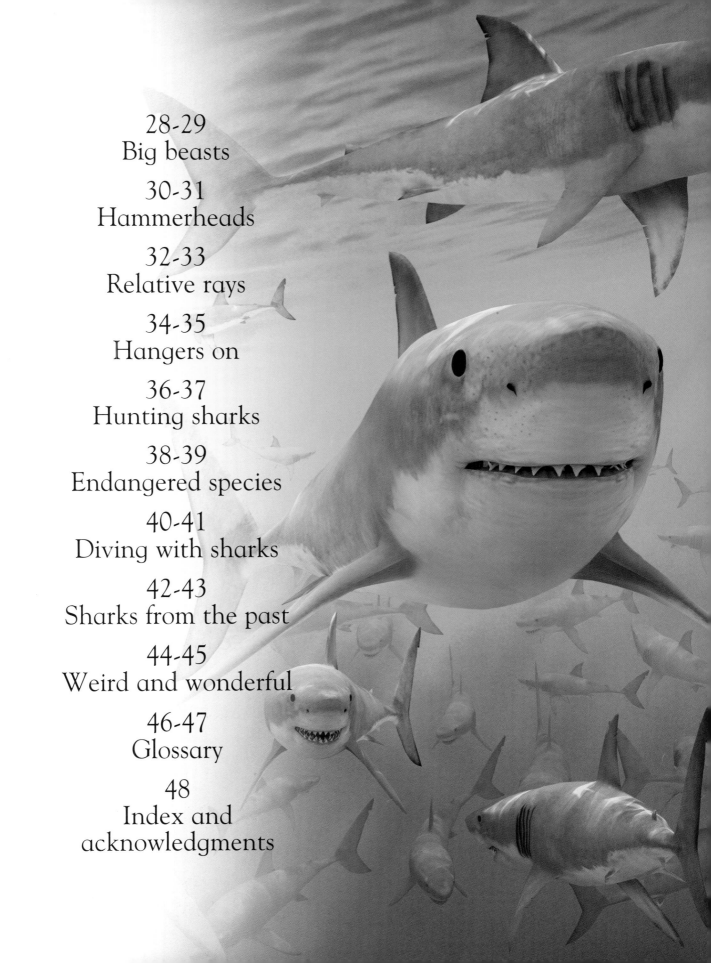

Introducing sharks

Sharks include the biggest fish in the sea—but not every species is huge, and most are not dangerous to people either. There are more than 500 different shark species, from the gigantic whale shark to the tiny dwarf lanternshark.

33 ft (10 m)

Basking shark

60 ft (18 m)

Whale shark

Gentle giants

Found in warm tropical waters, whale sharks cruise at about 2 mph (3 km/h). They can grow to 60 ft (18 m) long—so big, they sometimes bump into ships!

The pattern of spots on a whale shark

Shark facts

- Sharks live in every ocean in the world. A few species are found in rivers, too.

- Aside from humans, a shark's biggest enemy is another shark—many will eat their own species.

- Only about four people a year are killed by sharks.

Big sharks, little sharks

20 ft (6 m)

Great white shark

10 ft (3 m)
Nurse shark

Great hammerhead shark

Dwarf lanternshark
8 in (21 cm)

20 ft (6 m)

Tiger shark

Spinner shark
9 ft (2.8 m)

18 ft (5.5 m)

Brownbanded bamboo shark
3 ft 3 in (1 m)

is different on each individual.

Whale sharks
are harmless
to people.

The inside story

Sharks are not the same as bony fish such as cod and trout. Sharks are cartilaginous fish—they have skeletons made of cartilage.

Sharp skin

A shark's skin is rough, covered in sharp scales called denticles. It's a bit like having skin covered in teeth. As a shark grows, the denticles fall out and are replaced by bigger ones.

CAUDAL FIN
The caudal fin is the shark's tail. It is made up of two parts called lobes.

SECOND DORSAL FIN

ANAL FIN
Not all sharks have an anal fin.

PELVIC FIN
Pelvic and pectoral fins come in pairs. All other fins are unpaired.

STOMACH
Many sharks can turn their U-shaped stomachs inside out to throw up an unwanted meal.

Tail details

Some fast-swimming sharks have a keel on either side of their caudal fin, or tail. It is thought that this helps the tail move smoothly from side to side when the shark swims.

KEEL

Getting oxygen

Living underwater, sharks cannot breathe in air like people do. Instead, they take in water through the mouth. This passes over the shark's gills, which absorb oxygen from the water. The water then escapes through gill slits in the skin.

Most sharks have five gill slits.

DORSAL FIN
Sharks use their fins in different ways. The dorsal, pelvic, and anal fins stop the shark from rolling over.

VERTEBRAL COLUMN
Joined-up blocks of cartilage act as the shark's spine.

GILLS
Some sharks have an extra pair of gill openings called spiracles. These supply oxygen to the eyes and brain.

SNOUT

NOSTRIL
Sharks don't us their nostrils to breathe, just for smelling.

LIVER
The shark's liver is full of oil, which helps the shark's ability to float in the water.

PECTORAL FIN
This pair of fins steers and gives lift.

Sink or swim!

Bony fish have a swim bladder—an air sac that helps a fish to float or sink in the water. Sharks don't have swim bladders and must keep swimming so they don't sink. Basking sharks have such large, oil-filled livers they can swim slowly without sinking.

Cartilage is lighter and more flexible than bone

Skeleton made of bon

Heads...

Blunt snouts, pointed snouts, even one covered in teeth... Not every shark looks the same. In fact, nearly every species has its own head shape.

Sharp and sleek
Having a pointed snout gives this blue shark a streamlined shape for swimming.

A streamlined snout cuts through the water like

Eyes forward!
Some sharks have their mouths set back behind their eyes, such as the bull shark. Others, like the mako shark, have their mouths in front of their eyes. This difference is one of the features that scientists use to identify sharks.

They may be tiny, but the Port Jackson's teeth are sharp enough to hold onto prey.

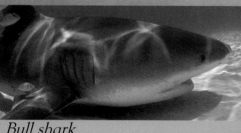

Bull shark

Mako shark

Pig head
With its blunt head and snout, it's easy to see why the Port Jackson shark is sometimes also called the "pig fish." The shark's huge nostrils help it sniff out prey such as shellfish and sea urchins.

a torpedo.

Feeling for food

Nurse sharks have feelers, called barbels, at the end of their snout. They use them to poke around on the seabed, feeling for food.

Saw shark

Barbel

Saw point

The very unusual-looking saw shark has a long, pointed snout with teeth that stick out on either side. Halfway down the snout are two long, flexible barbels.

Wide as a whale shark

The mouth of a whale shark is at the very end of its flat, wide snout. At 5 ft (1.5 m) wide, the shark's mouth is huge—but its eyes are tiny.

Eye protection

Some sharks, such as the hammerhead, have special "third eyelids." This membrane can cover and protect the eye while the shark thrashes around with prey in the water.

9

... And tails

Whether big or small, uneven or equal-sized, plain or patterned, all sharks' tails are powerful. Swinging from side to side, the tail creates lift as a shark swims along. It's a shark's driving force!

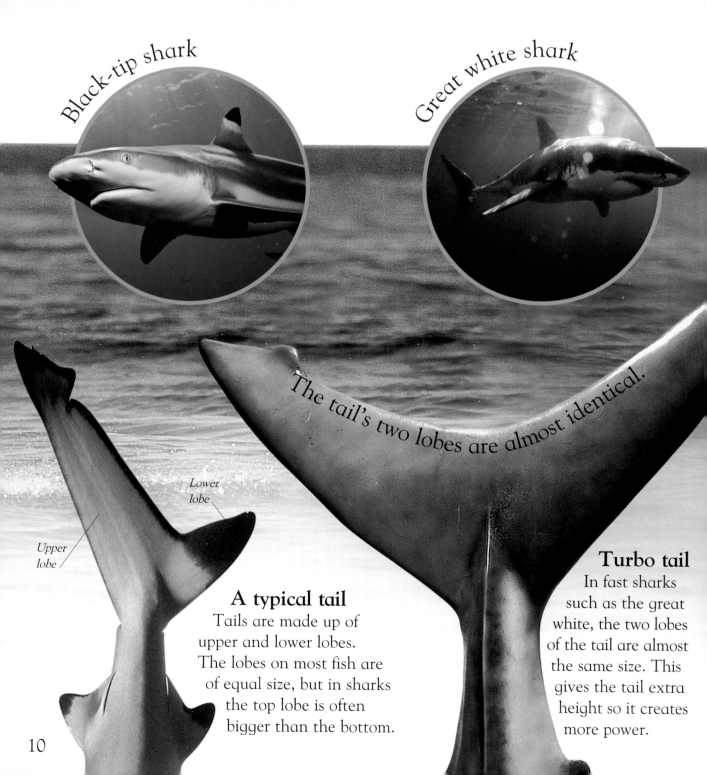

Black-tip shark

Great white shark

The tail's two lobes are almost identical.

Lower lobe

Upper lobe

A typical tail
Tails are made up of upper and lower lobes. The lobes on most fish are of equal size, but in sharks the top lobe is often bigger than the bottom.

Turbo tail
In fast sharks such as the great white, the two lobes of the tail are almost the same size. This gives the tail extra height so it creates more power.

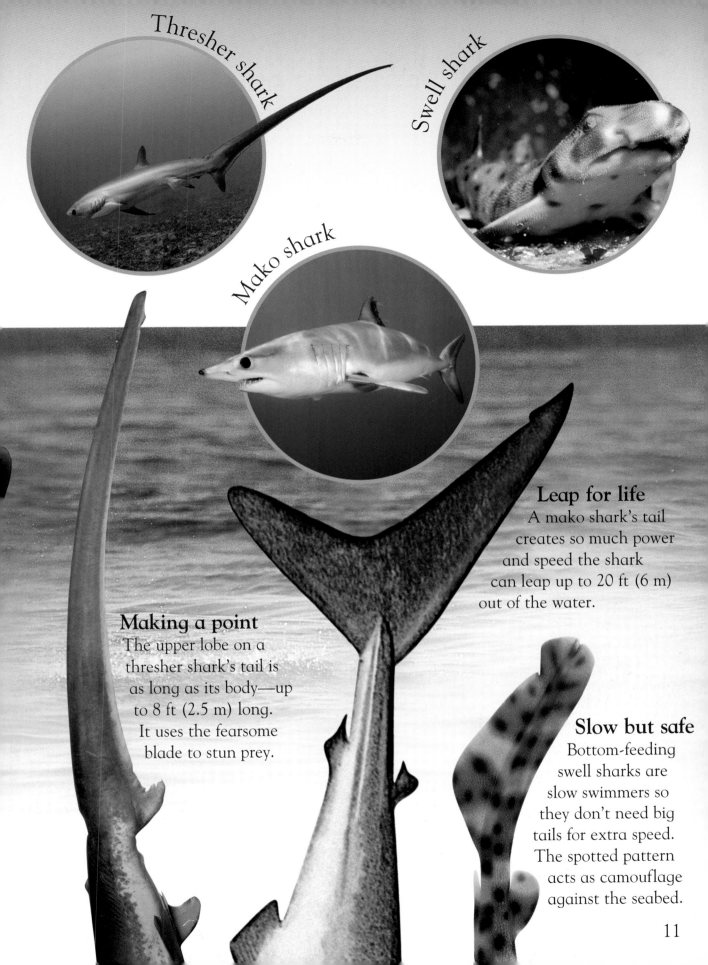

Thresher shark

Swell shark

Mako shark

Leap for life
A mako shark's tail creates so much power and speed the shark can leap up to 20 ft (6 m) out of the water.

Making a point
The upper lobe on a thresher shark's tail is as long as its body—up to 8 ft (2.5 m) long. It uses the fearsome blade to stun prey.

Slow but safe
Bottom-feeding swell sharks are slow swimmers so they don't need big tails for extra speed. The spotted pattern acts as camouflage against the seabed.

Super swimmers

Moving its tail left and right, a shark swims silently through the water. With the twitch of a fin, the shark changes direction. It may be hunting for food, seeking a breeding partner, or going on a long migration.

Changing the angle of the pectoral fins makes the shark turn left or right, and up or down.

Fantastic fins

Sharks need their fins in order to swim. The caudal fin, or tail, is very important. It is the shark's "engine"— it provides thrust (pushing power) and lift (to stop the shark from sinking).

Some sharks will suffocate if they don't keep swimming.

Caudal fin

No flapping!

Most bony fish can flap their fins, but sharks can't move their fins in the same way. They use their fins to provide lift, and like bony fish, to stop themselves from rolling, or for steering.

S is for swimming

As a shark swims, its body curves from side to side in an S-shape. The curve starts at the head and moves back along the body, getting larger toward the tail.

Breathing in water

As sharks swim, the flow of water in through the mouth and over the gills provides oxygen for the shark to survive. Nurse sharks spend lots of time resting on the seabed, so to get oxygen they use their cheek muscles to suck in water.

Who's the fastest?

If all sharks had a race, mako sharks would win: they can swim at 60 mph (97 km/h). Blue sharks would probably come second: over short distances, they can reach speeds of 43 mph (69 km/h).

Blue shark

If the two sharks chased the same prey, the mako would shoot forward and overtake the blue shark.

Mako shark

Swimming facts

● Sharks can't stop suddenly. They must move left or right to avoid collisions.

● Sharks can't swim backward.

● Small sharks bend more than large sharks when swimming.

Walking in water

Epaulette sharks don't just use their pectoral fins for swimming, but for walking, too! They pull themselves along the seabed with the fins while they search for food.

Lots of sense

Sharks have all the five senses that people do (seeing, hearing, smelling, tasting, and touching), plus an extra "electrical sense" that helps them find prey.

Cats also have a tapetum. It reflects light, which can make their eyes look shiny.

Special sight

Most sharks have good eyesight, and some can even see in color. Some sharks have a tapetum—a layer of special cells at the back of the eye that helps them to see in dim light.

It is thought that great white sharks can see in color.

Some sharks can sniff out a meal from more than half a mile

DO SHARKS HAVE EARS?

You can't see ears on a shark, but they do have ears inside their heads. Tiny openings in the shark's head, near its brain, pick up sounds that travel through the water. They can even tell which direction the noise is coming from, and from over half a mile (1 km) away.

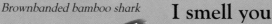

Brownbanded bamboo shark

I smell you

Sharks have a much better sense of smell than we do. As a shark swims along, water flows into its nostrils. If there's a fishy smell in the water, the shark will move its head from side to side to find the direction it's coming from. Then it may head off after its prey.

Long-distance touch

Just like people, sharks feel with their skin. Running down both sides of a shark's body is the "lateral line"—a line of cells that picks up vibrations, so sharks can feel if something is moving in the water, even from hundreds of yards away.

It's electrifying!

All living things give out weak electrical signals. Sharks can pick up these signals through pores on their snouts called ampullae of Lorenzini. Using this sense, sharks can detect prey hidden in the sand on the seabed.

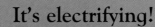

Ampullae of Lorenzini pores

(1 km) away.

Unlike a human tongue, a shark's small, thick tongue doesn't move very much.

A matter of taste

Sharks have tastebuds inside their mouths, but not on their tongues, like people do. Some sharks are fussy eaters and will spit out prey that they don't like—but it may be too late for the prey, which has already been bitten.

Jaws

All sharks are carnivorous (they eat meat). Most of them need powerful jaws and sharp teeth to kill their prey. The shape of the teeth depends on what the shark eats.

A tiger shark's jaws are so strong, it can bite through a turtle's shell.

Life-size sand tiger shark tooth

Life-size tiger shark tooth

Sharp as a needle

Sand tiger sharks have pointed teeth for holding onto slippery fish and squid. The uneven rows of curved, needle-sharp teeth give the sand tiger its other name: the ragged-tooth shark.

Terrifying teeth

With these fearsome teeth, tiger sharks are able to bite chunks out of almost anything. The sharp point stabs prey, while the jagged edges cut through the flesh of fish and any other animals found in the sea—even including people!

Life-size great white shark tooth

Double-edged saw

A great white shark has sharp, triangular teeth with serrated edges, like a saw. They are used for tearing prey such as sea mammals.

Shell-crushers

Many sharks that live on the seabed have flat teeth at the backs of their jaws that are used for crushing shellfish.

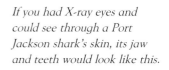

If you had X-ray eyes and could see through a Port Jackson shark's skin, its jaw and teeth would look like this.

A tiger shark breaks through the surface of the sea while chasing prey.

New teeth, please!

Have you ever lost a tooth? Sharks do, all the time. As soon as a front tooth is worn out or breaks, it is replaced by one in the row behind. Sharks can go through thousands of teeth in a lifetime.

Toothy facts

● Sharks may have up to 3,000 teeth at one time. The biggest teeth are at the front.

● Sharks can push their jaws forward away from the skull to take much bigger bites than normal.

● Tiger sharks can grow 24,000 teeth in 10 years.

Tiny teeth

Basking sharks are filter feeders— they swallow huge amounts of plankton that live in seawater. The plankton are so small, the shark doesn't need to bite or chew them, so its teeth are hardly used.

Feeding frenzy

A reef shark picks up the scent of wounded fish in the water. He swims to his prey—but he's not the only shark at the scene. If there is plenty of food around, it could turn into a feeding frenzy!

A swell surprise
Some sharks catch their prey by ambushing it. Swell sharks hide on the seabed until a fish swims past... then they spring open their jaws and gulp the fish down.

So many sharks
Feeding frenzies don't often happen in the wild, but if lots of sharks detect the same scent or movement of prey in the water, they may all end up at the same feeding ground. If there's lots of food, the sharks jostle each other in a feeding frenzy.

Sharks go for injured prey

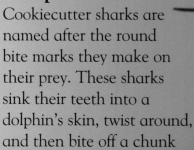

Sharp cookie
Cookiecutter sharks are named after the round bite marks they make on their prey. These sharks sink their teeth into a dolphin's skin, twist around, and then bite off a chunk of flesh to eat.

The hunt is on

While some sharks sneak up on their prey, others are more brazen predators. Fast sharks can catch prey after a high-speed chase. Some sharks may also feast on "bait balls." Diving into the bait ball breaks up the fish that pack together for protection.

A blue shark tackles a swarm of krill, which are tiny, shrimplike animals.

On the menu

However they catch it, all sharks eat meat. Fish and shellfish are the main part of most sharks' diet, but some eat seals, sealions, and seabirds, too. Larger sharks may also feast on their smaller cousins.

over healthy prey because it's easier to catch.

Stingray

Gannet

Fur seal

Turtle

Sardines

Squid

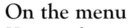

STOMACH THAT!

Tiger sharks are the garbage cans of the sea, hunting prey and scavenging for anything they can find. Scientists have found some very strange "food" in tiger sharks' stomachs. Stingrays and squid sound quite edible, but tin cans, animal antlers, shoes, car license plates, car tires, handbags, and a human hand are not recommended for lunch!

Bottom feeders

Sharks that hunt on or near the ocean floor are known as bottom feeders. Often slow-moving, these sharks probe the seabed for unsuspecting prey, or simply wait for it to come to them.

Angel ambush

Some angel sharks hunt at night, swimming quite far in their search for fish and shellfish. But most angel sharks feed during the day, resting on the seabed and lying in wait for their prey. When a fish swims past, the shark lifts its head and snaps up the prey with its sharp teeth.

Hide and seek

With its flat body and sandy-colored skin, the angel shark is perfect at hiding on the seabed—even though it can grow to nearly 6½ ft (2 m) long! It uses its extra-large pectoral fins to dig down into the sand.

Angel sharks have eyes on the tops of their heads so they can see while resting.

An ambushing angel shark rears up like a cobra.

Now you see me...

Swell sharks hide in rocky crevices and caves during the day, the pattern on their skin blending in with the stony seabed. The camouflage helps them hide from predators— as slow swimmers, they might not be able to escape a large, hungry shark.

... Now you don't

Even more camouflaged than a swell shark, a wobbegong settles down among coral. It has fringes of skin around its mouth that look like seaweed. Wobbegongs live along coastlines and have sometimes been stepped on by swimmers who can't see them.

Finding food

Hidden among the sand and stones on the seabed are lots of fish and other sea creatures that sharks like to eat—but first they need to find them. They may use their electrical sense, their sense of smell, or, like this epaulette shark, their barbels to poke around in the sand to sense prey.

I saw the prey

Saw sharks often feed on the bottom, skimming their "saw" across the surface of the seabed to disturb creatures. They have long barbels for sensing prey on the surface.

21

Migration

Some sharks like to live in cool water, others in warm water. When summer turns to winter, or winter to summer, the water temperature changes. This is when many sharks migrate.

ALASKA

SCOTLAND

CANADA

A basking shark that lived near Scotland swam 5,958 miles (9,589 km) across the Atlantic Ocean to Newfoundland, Canada.

HAWAIIAN ISLANDS

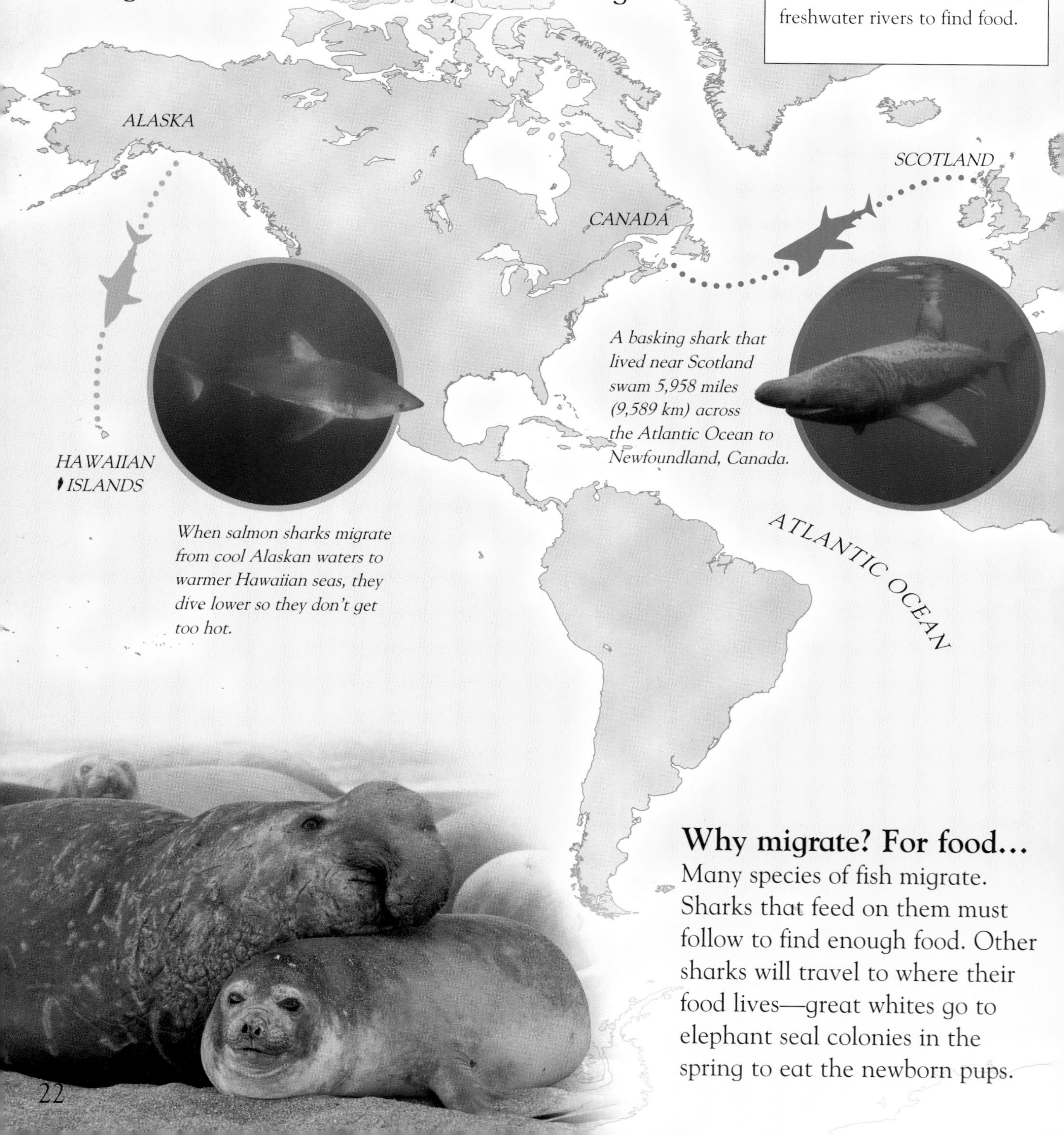

When salmon sharks migrate from cool Alaskan waters to warmer Hawaiian seas, they dive lower so they don't get too hot.

ATLANTIC OCEAN

Why migrate? For food...

Many species of fish migrate. Sharks that feed on them must follow to find enough food. Other sharks will travel to where their food lives—great whites go to elephant seal colonies in the spring to eat the newborn pups.

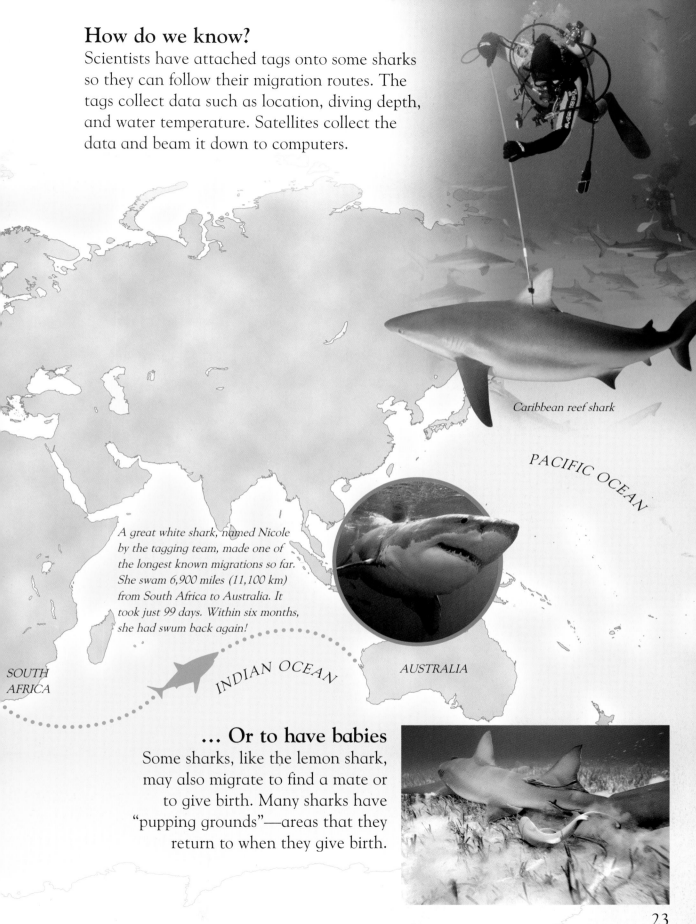

How do we know?

Scientists have attached tags onto some sharks so they can follow their migration routes. The tags collect data such as location, diving depth, and water temperature. Satellites collect the data and beam it down to computers.

Caribbean reef shark

PACIFIC OCEAN

A great white shark, named Nicole by the tagging team, made one of the longest known migrations so far. She swam 6,900 miles (11,100 km) from South Africa to Australia. It took just 99 days. Within six months, she had swum back again!

SOUTH AFRICA

INDIAN OCEAN

AUSTRALIA

... Or to have babies

Some sharks, like the lemon shark, may also migrate to find a mate or to give birth. Many sharks have "pupping grounds"—areas that they return to when they give birth.

23

Young sharks

Birds lay eggs, mammals give birth to live young, and sharks… Well, that depends on the species. Some give birth to live young, and some lay eggs.

Mermaid's purses

Some dogfish eggs look like leathery bags, which are sometimes called "mermaid's purses." Tendrils at the top and bottom wrap around seaweed to stop the eggs from being swept away by ocean currents.

Newly laid soft eggs soon turn hard in the water.

Inside an egg

Sharks' eggs look nothing like birds' eggs, but inside, similar things are happening…

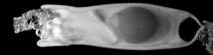

1. Inside the leathery case of a lesser spotted dogfish egg, an embryo starts to form. It is attached to a yolk sac, which contains its food.

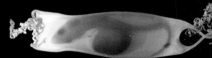

2. As it uses up its food, the embryo grows and the yolk shrinks. Water seeps through the egg case, providing oxygen to keep the embryo alive.

3. Eight to nine months after the egg was laid, the dogfish hatches. All sharks are born looking like small versions of adult sharks. Unlike most bony fish, they do not have to change body shape (called metamorphosis) into an adult.

Baby sharks are called pups.

Scrambled egg

Horn sharks lay spiral-shaped eggs. The unusual shape is useful for wedging among underwater rocks, so the eggs aren't washed away.

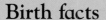

Birth facts

- Lesser spotted dogfish are 4 in (10 cm) long when they hatch.

- Lemon sharks can give birth to up to 17 pups in one litter…

- … But hammerheads might produce up to 40 pups at once.

Live young

Some shark species develop in a similar way to people: they grow inside their mothers, connected by an umbilical cord. The cord breaks from the mother when the pup is born.

Lemon sharks

The egg contains all the nutrients this shark needs to grow in the womb.

Egg for breakfast

Most pups develop inside eggs but hatch while they are still inside their mother, so she gives birth to live young. Some sharks, such as spiny dogfish, are born still attached to their egg. They absorb the food from the yolk until it is all used up.

A shark can swim and hunt for food as soon as it is born.

Bye, Mom!

Lemon sharks give birth in shallow water. The pups come out tail first, and then swim off. Like all shark species, they are not cared for by their mothers: they must fend for themselves from the moment they are born.

Attack!

The great white shark sits at the top of the food chain. The 21 ft- (6.5 m-) long predator is dangerous to large fish and hunts mammals such as seals, sea lions, and dolphins. It may also attack humans, though this is rare.

Now you see me
What color is a white shark? Mostly silver gray! Any prey looking up from the bottom of the sea would not see the pale belly of the shark, since it blends in with the sunlight reflecting on the surface of the sea.

A burst of speed and the seal is caught.

It's an ambush!
A great white can't change direction very quickly, so to be a successful hunter, it must surprise its prey. It normally cruises along at a gentle 2 mph (3 km/h), but when it finds prey, the shark shoots forward at 15 mph (25 km/h).

It's thought that most shark attacks on people are really a case of mistaken identity. Seen from below, a surfer on a board looks a lot like a seal—the shark's intended prey.

Watch out in the water
Is the great white really as dangerous as the film *Jaws* made out? They may kill more people than any other shark species—but attacks don't happen often. More people are killed by jellyfish.

Big beasts

The whale shark and basking shark are the two largest fish in the world. They may be huge, but they're harmless— unless you're plankton.

A basking shark's gill rakers are long bristles coated in slime.

Sieves of the sea

Basking sharks are filter feeders that eat plankton. They swim with their mouths open, taking in water. As the water flows out through the shark's gills, the plankton get trapped in gill rakers.

Hot food

On sunny days, basking sharks can be seen near the surface of the sea. They are following the plankton, which gather in warm, sunlit water.

28

The vacuum cleaner of the sea

A basking shark needs to swim to take in water, but a whale shark simply opens its huge mouth to suck in water. It can filter 1,600 gallons (6,000 liters) of water in an hour—that's the same amount of liquid that is in more than 18,000 cans of soda!

Small fish and squid are easily sucked into the shark's massive mouth.

A whale shark closes its mouth to swallow food. It can spit out food it doesn't like.

Plankton is made up of tiny sea creatures and algae.

Safety patrol

Schools of medium-size fish often attract predators, but this whale shark is no threat to them. The fish have chosen to gather around it because its huge size will stop other sharks from attacking them.

29

Scalloped hammerhead

Hammerheads

Scientists can only guess at the reasons behind the hammerhead's uniquely shaped head—but it probably gives the shark super hunting skills.

Big brother

There are eight different hammerhead species. Great hammerheads are the biggest, at 20 ft (6 m) long. At just 3 ft (90 cm) long, mallethead sharks are the smallest.

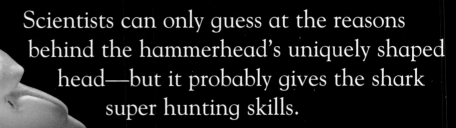

The shark's nostrils are near the ends of its head, effectively giving the shark a big nose! Its sense of smell is thought to be 10 times better than in other sharks.

Nostril

The shark's eyes are at the very ends of its wide head. As it swims, the shark turns its head from side to side so it can see all around.

Big head

Scalloped hammerhead sharks have distinctive dents in the front edge of their heads. These are the most commonly seen of all hammerheads.

Time for school

During the day, scalloped hammerheads sometimes gather in large schools. Nobody knows why they do this. When night falls, they go off by themselves to hunt for food.

Hammerhead facts

● These sharks like to live in warm waters around the coast.

● Many hammerheads migrate huge distances to reach feeding or breeding grounds.

● The shark's wide, flat head may act like a wing, giving the shark lift as it swims along.

Daring dentist

Carnivorous sharks can make friends! A barberfish eats food left in the shark's teeth, but it's not in danger: it keeps the shark clean, so it's left alone to do its job— and gets a free meal!

Is this the strangest shark in the sea?

Hungry hunters

Hammerheads eat all kinds of fish, including stingrays and even other sharks. They will attack turtles if given the opportunity, snapping off a flipper as a snack.

Relative rays

In the fish family tree, the nearest relatives to sharks are rays. As with sharks, their skeletons are made of cartilage, not bone.

Some stingrays have as many as seven spines on their tails.

Stingray

Most rays are not dangerous—but stingrays come with a deadly weapon: a razor-sharp spine that grows out of its tail. They use this in defense against predators, injecting them with poison that comes from a gland below the spine.

Fish with wings

Unlike sharks, most rays do not swim by waving their tails— they're too small and spindly. Instead, they flap their pectoral fins up and down. The fins are also known as wings.

Manta ray

How to spot a ray

Rays are often spotted or patterned to blend in with the seabed. Their eyes are on the tops of their heads, but their mouths are underneath.

Eagle rays

Most stingrays like to live in shallow water.

Distant cousin

Chimaeras are also cartilaginous fish. They have a very sharp dorsal fin, which can cause injury to people. A long, pointed tail gives this chimaera its other name: ratfish.

A TASTE FOR SHARP FOOD

With their sharp, poisonous spines, who would want to eat stingrays? Hammerhead sharks! Stingrays are among their favorite food, and the spines don't seem to hurt them. Some great hammerheads have been found with more than 50 spines embedded in the mouth and throat.

Hangers on

Who would want to hang around with killer sharks? There are some fish that like to: remoras use them to hitch a ride, and pilot fish like their big bodyguards. But other small hitchhikers are not so friendly.

Using its head

Remoras can swim for themselves, but why make the effort when they can get a lift from a shark or ray? The hard pad on top of a remora's head acts as a sucker for gripping onto the shark.

You scratch my back...

Remoras return the favor to their hosts by cleaning them—they eat the itchy parasites that live on the shark's skin. However, they also steal a few scraps from the shark's meal, too!

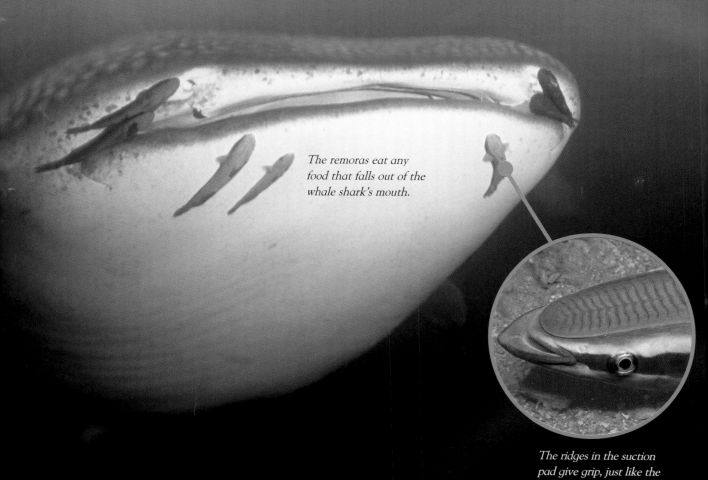

The remoras eat any food that falls out of the whale shark's mouth.

The ridges in the suction pad give grip, just like the

You can't catch me!

Pilot fish like to swim with sharks. These small fish may swim with larger sharks because it stops other predators from attacking them. The shark won't harm them either: they're too quick to be caught.

Pilot fish feed on the shark's parasites—and its dung!

Streaming behind

It's not just fish that hang around with sharks. Copepods are crustaceans (like crabs and lobsters). Some stick onto sharks' fins, and the females may trail long egg cases behind them. The young hatch into the water.

Female copepods often have darker shells than the males.

THE STORY OF A TAPEWORM

Tapeworms more than 3 ft (1 m) long can live inside a shark's gut, absorbing food. But how do they get there? A tapeworm lays eggs, which the shark passes into the sea. A copepod eats the eggs, which hatch, and then a bony fish eats the copepod. Finally, a shark eats the bony fish—baby tapeworm and all.

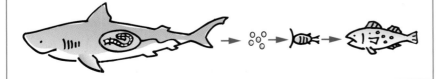

Not so friendly

Another type of copepod chooses to live in the eye of a Greenland shark. It comes to feed on the eye, but can't swim away again. It stops the shark from being able to see properly.

Hunting sharks

Sharks' flesh, fins, skin, teeth, and oil are used in all kinds of things that many people want, from food to jewelry. Every year, tens of millions of sharks are killed to satisfy our demands.

A sad ending

Most sharks are caught just for their fins. Some are "finned" while still alive, then thrown back into the sea. Unable to swim, they drown or are killed by predators.

An essential ingredient?

Stripped of skin and rubbed with salt, shark flesh is hung up to dry in the sun. In poorer countries, shark meat can provide important protein. But in some other countries, fresh shark meat is sold in markets alongside other fish.

Mako shark steaks are sold in some supermarkets.

Steak or soup?

In some parts of Europe and North and South America, shark meat is sold as a delicacy. In China, giving a guest shark fin soup is a great honor—but not for the shark. Around 100 different species are caught for their fins, used in making the soup.

Shark-fin soup

Greenland shark meat is popular in northern Europe.

Necklace made from shark's teeth

Unlucky charm

Some people like to wear shark-tooth jewelry, such as necklaces. They think it makes them look as scary as a shark, or that it brings them good luck.

Trading teeth

Shark jaws are sold as souvenirs in many beach resorts, but you might be breaking the law to bring one home. Some species can only be sold internationally if the seller has a special permit.

Endangered species

Sharks are important animals: they help maintain a balance of other fish and animals in the oceans. But sharks are in trouble. More than 100 shark species are threatened, including great white, hammerhead, and whale sharks.

Smooth hammerhead

Off the menu

People are the biggest threat to sharks. Spiny dogfish was once very common in European waters, but so many have been caught for their meat that the species is now endangered. The shark meat is sold in UK fish-and-chip shops as "rock salmon."

A great expense

Almost all of the eight hammerhead species are at risk. Some are caught on purpose, others accidentally along with other fish. Their fins are among the most expensive of shark fins when sold.

How you can help

● Don't buy souvenirs made from shark products such as jaws and teeth.

● Eat fish that come from "sustainable populations"— species that are looked after so they are not overfished.

● Don't eat shark-fin soup.

Not enough pups

Many sharks, including sand tigers, give birth to only two pups every other year. This means that for some species, there are not enough pups being born to replace the sharks being caught.

A young sand tiger

Not very sportsmanlike

Rare gulper sharks are fished for their meat and oil—and on top of that, they are also hunted by anglers. Gulpers fight against the fishing line, which makes anglers want to catch one to show off their skills.

Long, drifting gill nets are illegal, but are still used in the Indian and Pacific oceans.

Bye-bye bycatch

Thresher sharks, among many other species, are at risk because they get caught as "bycatch"—caught in nets that are laid to catch other fish. Unable to swim away, they suffocate. They may be sold, finned, or thrown back into the sea.

A DYING BREED?

There are around 20 species of sharks known to be at risk of extinction—and possibly more that we don't know about. Ganges sharks are critically endangered. They have been over-fished, and their home—the Ganges River in India—is polluted. People have also built dams that stop the sharks from swimming freely.

Diving with sharks

Coming face to face with a shark can be terrifying. For surfers and swimmers, a hungry shark is the last thing they want to meet. But for some people, it's all in a day's work.

Cameras have special plastic cases to make them waterproof.

Divers use SCUBA gear to breathe underwater. The tanks contain air, which the diver breathes in through a regulator.

Diving cages can protect people from even the most dangerous shark

Studying sharks

Marine biologists are scientists who study sea life. They tag sharks to track them and learn about shark behavior.

1 A mako shark is lifted out of the sea to be tagged. A tube pumps water down its throat and over its gills to provide oxygen.

2 A tag is fitted to the shark's dorsal fin. It's thought this doesn't hurt the shark—it's a bit like having your ears pierced.

3 The cradle is lowered back into the sea and the shark swims away. The tag will record where the shark goes.

Come here!
Before someone can tag or photograph a shark, they need to find one. This can be tricky in a vast ocean, so people attract sharks using chum (chopped-up fish) or seal-shaped lures.

Behind bars
Scientists, photographers, and even tourists can dive in cages to get closer to sharks. Lured by bait, the shark will approach, but can't get in.

—the great white.

41

Sharks from the past

Sharks are even older than dinosaurs!
The first sharks swam the seas around
450 million years ago—long before reptiles,
birds, and mammals appeared on Earth.
(And 200 million years before the dinosaurs.)

In the beginning

With fossils dating back to 370
million years ago, *Cladoselache* is
thought to be one of the first sharks.
It was around 4 ft (1.2 m) long and
had a tail shape similar to that of a
mako or great white shark.

The Megalodon
*jaw is huge
compared to a
great white's jaw.*

*Great white
shark jaw*

*Life-size
Megalodon
tooth*

The big one

Possibly the most famous ancient shark
is the *Megalodon*, which lived from
around 20 million to 2 million years ago.
No whole *Megalodon* fossils have been found,
so we don't really know what it looked like.

*Based on the size
of its huge jaw,
it's thought that
Megalodon reached
52 ft (16 m) long.*

The modern ones

Some scientists think catsharks, bullheads, and cow sharks are closely related to the earliest modern sharks, which first appeared 200 million years ago.

This catshark fossil shows that modern catsharks haven't changed much.

The spiked one

This prickly character, called *Stethacanthus*, lived around 300 million years ago. The spiny denticles on its head may have been used in defense. The 6 ft- (2m-) long shark would certainly be a difficult meal to swallow.

This model shows how Stethacanthus may have looked.

How Fossils Form

Paleontologists (scientists who study the past) use fossils to learn about life in ancient times. Shark fossils form when a dead shark at the bottom of the sea gets covered in sand and mud. The soft parts rot away, but the harder parts, such as teeth, remain. Over time, the mud turns to rock. The shark's remains are replaced by minerals, forming a fossil.

The shark dies...   *... and gets buried.*   *The teeth fossilize.*

Finding fossils

Around 3,000 extinct kinds of shark are known from discovered fossils. Many have been found on land, which in ancient times would have been under water. Lots of fossils are of teeth, but the oldest ones are of skin denticles.

In this book you will have seen big sharks, powerful sharks, and sharks with fearsome teeth. But down in the deepest waters of the ocean are perhaps the strangest sharks of all.

Gruesome goblin

Goblin sharks wouldn't win any beauty contests! This rare shark is the only species to have a snout that sticks out from its forehead.

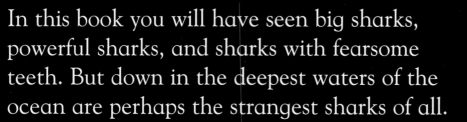

It's frilling!

Frilled sharks live up to 5,000 ft (1,500 m) below the surface of the ocean. With its long, thin body and gills that look like frills, it looks a little like a scary eel.

Odd ones out

Wobbegongs live on the seabed in shallow water. Some species have tassles of skin that look like seaweed. Together with a flat body and bulging eyes, they look like no other shark in the sea.

Well traveled

Cookiecutter sharks leave bite marks of perfect circles on their prey. Some travel from the ocean depths to the surface at night to feed. That's a return trip of up to 4½ miles (7 km) every day.

The first megamouth was discovered just over 30 years ago.

Big at the top

Not all strange sharks live deep in the water. Megamouths probably live only 500 ft (150 m) down. They are so rare, only a few of these big—and big-mouthed—sharks have ever been seen.

Velvetbelly lanternsharks may glow to find each other or to attract mates.

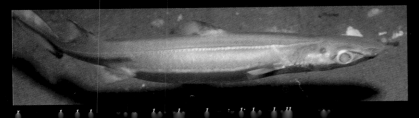

Lighting the way

It's dark in the ocean depths, but the world's smallest sharks can still be seen. Lanternsharks have special cells in their bodies that glow in the dark.

Glossary

Here are the meanings of some words it is useful to know when learning about sharks.

Ampullae of Lorenzini tiny sensors on a shark's snout that pick up electrical signals in the water. Sharks use them to find prey, and possibly to sense Earth's magnetic field to help them find their way in the sea.

Bait ball a school of fish that is targeted as prey by a shark or other predator.

Barbel a feeler that some sharks have on their snouts, used for probing the seabed to find food.

Buoyancy the ability to float. Sharks have oil-filled livers to help their buoyancy.

Bycatch sharks and other sea creatures that accidentally get caught in fishing nets that have been laid for other fish.

Camouflage a color or pattern that blends in with its surroundings, so it can't be seen.

Carnivore an animal that eats only meat.

Cartilage gristlelike tissue inside animal bodies that is lighter and more flexible than bone.

Cartilaginous fish that have skeletons made of cartilage.

Caudal fin the shark's tail.

Chum a smelly liquid used to attract sharks. It is made from mashed fish.

Copepod a type of crustacean. There are thousands of different copepod species, some of which live on sharks' bodies.

Crustacean a type of animal with jointed legs, but without a backbone. They usually have hard outer shells. Copepods, krill, and crabs are crustaceans.

Denticles scales that cover a shark's skin. They are toothlike and not like those on bony fish.

Dorsal fin a large fin in the middle of a shark's back that helps stop the shark from rolling over. Some sharks also have a second, smaller dorsal fin near their tail.

Embryo an unborn animal that is developing inside its mother's womb or in an egg.

Endangered species a species that is in danger of becoming extinct. Critically endangered species (such as Ganges sharks) are in immediate danger of dying out if things do not change.

Extinct a species that has died out. *Megalodon* sharks are extinct.

Filter feeder sharks that take in huge amounts of seawater as they swim along and filter out food contained in the water.

Finning chopping the fins off sharks to sell them. Often the shark is thrown back into the sea, where it will die.

Fossil the remains of an ancient animal or plant that have been preserved in rock.

Gills the part of a shark's body that absorbs oxygen from the water that the shark breathes in.

Gill rakers long bristles that filter feeders use to sieve food from the water they take in.

Gill slits openings in the shark's skin where water flows out. Most sharks have five gill slits.

Lateral line a line of cells along the sides of a shark that are sensitive to pressure and can detect movement in the water.

Migration moving from one place to another when seasons change. Some migrations involve very long journeys.

Oxygen a gas that is found in air and water. Most living things need oxygen to survive.

Parasite an animal that lives on or in another animal and takes food from its host.

Pectoral fin one of a pair of fins under the front of a shark's body, used to steer and give lift.

Pelvic fin one of a pair of fins under the rear of a shark's body, used to help stop the shark from rolling.

Plankton tiny animals, plants, and algae that drift in the ocean. They are eaten by many larger animals.

Predator an animal that hunts, kills, and eats another animal.

Prey an animal that is hunted, killed, and eaten by a predator.

Pup a baby shark.

Pupping ground an area where sharks gather to give birth.

Scavenger an animal that searches for food scraps, rather than hunting prey. Scavengers often eat the remains of animals killed by others.

School (of fish) a large number of fish that swim together.

SCUBA diving diving with air tanks. "SCUBA" stands for Self-Contained Underwater Breathing Apparatus.

Snout the front part of a shark's head.

Species a group of animals or plants of the same type that can produce young together.

Spiracles an extra pair of gill openings that supply oxygen to the shark's eyes and brain.

Streamlined a smooth shape that allows some sharks to swim faster.

Swim bladder an air sac inside bony fish that they can fill with air to help them float. Sharks do not have a swim bladder.

Tapetum a layer of cells at the back of a shark's eye that reflects light, helping it to see in the dark.

Umbilical cord a tube that connects an embryo to a placenta. The placenta absorbs oxygen and nutrients from the mother's blood to supply the embryo.

Index

Acknowledgments

Dorling Kindersley would like to thank:
Andy Cooke for original artwork, Sadie Thomas, Mary Sandberg, and Katie Newman for design assistance, Simon Mumford for cartography, and Rob Nunn, Claire Bowers, and Emma Shepherd in the DK Picture Library.

Picture credits

The publisher would like to thank the following for their kind permission to reproduce their photographs:
a=above; c=center; b=below; l=left; r=right; t=top

Alamy Images: Mark Conlin 19t, 39br; Chris A Crumley 9tl; Ethan Daniels 21cr; David Fleetham 10tr, 26t, 44b; Geoffrey Kidd 16cr; Jeff Rotman 4-5, 25cl; Visual & Written SL 41t; **Ardea:** Ken Lucas 13br; **Corbis:** Amos Nachoum 8t, 13c, 13t; Ralph A. Clevenger 19br; Clouds Hill Imaging Ltd 6t; Brandon D Cole 33br; Tim Davis 26b; Douglas P. Wilson / Frank Lane Picture Agency 24c, 24cb, 24cr; Stephen Frink 8cl, 34bl; image100 25; Momatiuk-Eastcott 22b; Louie Psihoyos 42br; Jeffrey L Rotman 2cla, 8cr, 9cr; Jeffrey L. Rotman 17cr, 37br, 40-41; Denis Scott 2-3; Paul Souders 19cl, 19crb; **DK Images:** Colin Keates / Courtesy of the Natural History Museum, London 16-17, 48tc; Harry Taylor / Courtesy of the Natural History Museum, London 16bc, 17bc, 17tc, 17tr, 42bl, 43c; Mike Row (c) The British Museum 37bl; Richard Davies of Oxford Scientific Films 12bc, 12bl, 12br; **The Field Museum:** Karen Carr 43cr;

FLPA: Mike Parry 1; Norbert Wu 35c, 36b, 36tc; **Getty Images:** altrendo images 8-9t; Brandon Cole / VIsuals Unlimited 38b; Bill Curtsinger / National Geographic 45t; Stephen Frink 10tl, 16bl; Larry Gatz 12-13; George Grall 16tl; Ken Lucas 15ca; David Nardini 23c; Benne Ochs 15bl; Rich Reid 19cra; Jeff Rotman 15br; Brian Skerry / National Geographic 18-19; Paul Souders 19c; Darryl Torckler 48; Mark Webster 22tr; David Wrobel 8-9b; **Hunterian Museum:** Hunterian Museum & Art Gallery, University of Glasgow 43cb; **imagequestmarine.com:** Kelvin Aiken / V & W 9tr, 20br; Mark Conlin-VWPics.com 40bc, 40bl, 40br; Klaus Jost 19cr; Andy Murch / V&W 21t; Andre Seale 33tc; Jez Tryner 29br; Masa Ushioda 32br; Dray van Beeck 35t; James D. Watt 33tr, 34t; **iStockphoto.com:** Robert Dant 16ca; **naturepl.com:** Brandon Cole 11c; Doug Perrine 8bl, 9br; Georgette Douwma 24br; Florian Graner 45bl; Alan James 28t; Nature Production 24bl; Jeff Rotman 27bl, 30tl; **NHPA / Photoshot:** Michael Patrick O'Neill 34br; Tom & Therisa Stack 32-33; **Photolibrary:** Dave Fleetham 6-7c; OSF / Howard Hall 17br; Paulo De Oliveira / OSF 44tr; **SeaPics.com:** 18cl, 18t, 29bl, 29c, 29t, 31c, 38c, 39cl, 39t; George W. Benz 37tr; Marc Bernardi 31bl; Bob Cranston 31t; Doc White 6b, 46-47; Doug Perrine 11tl, 14cr, 17cla, 23b, 23tr, 25b, 25tr; David Fleetham 30tr; Florian Graner 43t; Tom Haight 45c; Makoto Hirose / e-Photography 20tr; Makoto Kubo / e-Photography 21br; D. W. Miller 42tl; Espen Redkal 45cb; Jeff Rotman 7t, 30b; David Shen 44cl; Jeremy Stafford-Deitsch 21cl; Mark Strickland 22t; Masa Ushioda 37tl; James D. Watt 14-15, 31b; David Wrobel 11tr; **Still Pictures:** Klaus Jost 27t

Jacket images: *Front:* Getty Images t. naturepl.com: Jeff Rotman bl. SeaPics.com: bc, br. *Back:* **Corbis:** Paul Souders.

All other images © Dorling Kindersley

For further information see: www.dkimages.com